SINEAD O'CONNOR

The Biography - Career Downfall, Relationships, and Life Challenges Faced by the Artist who Tore up a Picture of Pope John Paul II in 1992

CHARLES KENNY

SINEAD O'CONNOR

Copyright © 2023 by Charles Kenny

All rights reserved. No part of this publication may be reproduced, distributed, or transmitted in any form or by any means, including photocopying, recording, or other electronic or mechanical methods, without the prior written permission of the publisher, except in the case of brief quotations embodied in critical reviews and certain other noncommercial uses permitted by copyright law.

DEDICATION

In dedication to Sinead O'Connor, her remarkable voice and unyielding spirit continue to resonate in the hearts of countless admirers worldwide. Through her music, she fearlessly challenged societal norms and advocated for social justice, leaving an indelible mark on the industry.

Her candidness about mental health struggles inspired empathy and opened vital conversations. A trailblazing artist and activist, she used her platform to elevate marginalized voices and foster positive change. As we remember her enduring legacy, may her unwavering courage and unwavering authenticity continue to inspire generations to come. Rest in peace, Sinead O'Connor.

TABLE OF CONTENT

INTRODUCTION

CHAPTER ONE

  Early Life and Beginning

CHAPTER TWO

  Music Career

CHAPTER THREE

  Awards and Achievements

CHAPTER FOUR

  Relationships and Personal Life

CHAPTER FIVE

  Life in Politics and Activism

CHAPTER SIX

  Controversies and Public Outbursts

CHAPTER SEVEN

  Personal Struggles

CHAPTER EIGHT

  Sinead O'Connor Passes

CHAPTER NINE

  Legacy and Impact

INTRODUCTION

In the roaring thunder of the music industry, few voices have reverberated with the unyielding power and raw emotion of Sinead O'Connor. From the moment she burst onto the scene, her haunting melodies and soul-stirring lyrics penetrated the hearts of millions, cementing her status as a true musical icon.

But behind the curtain of fame and adoration lay a tumultuous tale of triumph, controversy, and unyielding resilience that shaped the life of this extraordinary artist.

Born in the enchanting landscapes of Glenageary, County Dublin, Ireland, Sinead O'Connor's journey began like a whisper, a melody waiting to be sung. Her childhood reverberated with the echoes of music, a passion instilled by her family's harmonious love for the art. Yet, her path to stardom was not paved with gold; it was one of perseverance through personal struggles and societal battles.

In 1990, the world stood captivated as O'Connor soared to unimaginable heights with the release of her album "I Do Not Want What I Haven't Got." The ethereal ballad, "Nothing Compares 2 U," became an anthem of heartache, her voice a transcendent vessel of sorrow and vulnerability. But, it was this same voice that would lead her to a collision with controversy, shaking the very foundations of her career.

In 1992, O'Connor's defiance reached a crescendo on the hallowed stage of "Saturday Night Live." In an act of protest against an institution marred by scandal, she tore up a picture of Pope John Paul II, a moment that resounded across the globe like thunderclaps on a stormy night. The repercussions were profound, propelling her into the eye of a media hurricane that threatened to engulf her.

Yet, amidst the tempest, O'Connor proved to be an unyielding force of nature. Her artistry became the beacon that illuminated the darkness of her struggles with mental health, a battle she never shied away from. She wore her heart on her sleeve, baring her soul through music, activism, and candid revelations about her own demons.

In the shadows of personal turmoil and the heart-wrenching loss of her son Shane, who succumbed to the same darkness that haunted her, Sinead O'Connor's resilience shone like a supernova. Her voice, once again, transformed into an instrument of healing, reaching out to those grappling with their own pain, offering solace in shared vulnerability.

As we embark on this journey through the life of Sinead O'Connor, we find ourselves entangled in the tapestry of a remarkable soul, whose artistry dared to defy convention and whose spirit soared unapologetically. This biography is not merely a retelling of events but an exploration of a woman who danced fearlessly through the storms, leaving an indelible mark on the world.

Let delve into the triumphs, the controversies, and the unyielding resilience of an artist whose voice soared to the heavens, forever capturing the hearts of those who dared to listen. This is the story of Sinead O'Connor, a tale that echoes the triumph of the human spirit amidst the darkest of nights.

CHAPTER ONE

Early Life and Beginning

In the quaint town of Glenageary, County Dublin, Ireland, a star was born on December 8, 1966. Sinéad Marie Bernadette O'Connor, the third of five children, entered the world into a family marked by both love and challenges.

Sinéad's parents, Sean O'Connor and Marie O'Connor, had a tumultuous relationship, which eventually led to their separation when she was just eight years old. The dissolution of her parents' marriage left a profound impact on young Sinéad, shaping her perceptions of love and family from an early age.

Growing up in a household that struggled financially, Sinéad's childhood was far from idyllic. However, within those humble walls, her love for music blossomed. Encouraged by her mother, Marie, who was an amateur singer herself, Sinéad found solace and joy in singing, using her voice as a refuge from the world's uncertainties.

Her musical journey was further enriched by the eclectic tastes of her father, Sean, who introduced her to an array of genres, from traditional Irish folk to American blues. These diverse influences would later manifest in her distinct and powerful vocal style, setting her apart from her contemporaries.

Despite the hardships, the O'Connor family was a close-knit unit, bound by a deep sense of love and support. Sinéad's siblings, Joseph, Eimear, John, and Eoin, formed an essential part of her formative years, with whom she shared both laughter and tears.

As a teenager, Sinéad attended a Catholic convent school, where her rebellious spirit often clashed with the rigid traditions of the institution. Her nonconformist nature was evident even then, foreshadowing the fierce individuality that would define her later career.

CHAPTER TWO

Music Career

Sinéad O'Connor's music career was a testament to the power of raw talent and a voice that could stir souls. It was a journey that began with humble dreams in her hometown of Glenageary, Ireland, and eventually catapulted her to international fame.

With a burning desire to share her gift with the world, Sinéad embarked on her musical journey in her late teens. She honed her skills by performing in local venues and cafes, where her powerful voice and emotive performances started to attract attention. It was clear that this young Irish songstress possessed a rare ability to reach deep into the hearts of her audience.

In 1985, her dedication paid off when she caught the eye of Ensign Records, leading to the release of her debut album, "The Lion and the Cobra." The album showcased her distinct vocal style and the raw emotion that would become her signature. Critics lauded her as a fresh and compelling voice in the music industry.

However, it was her second studio album, "I Do Not Want What I Haven't Got," released in 1990, that truly solidified her position as a global sensation. The album featured her iconic rendition of the song "Nothing Compares 2 U," originally written by Prince. Sinéad's hauntingly beautiful performance struck a chord with millions, transcending genres and cultural boundaries.

The song's accompanying music video, with her

tearful face filling the screen, became an iconic image that captured the world's attention. "Nothing Compares 2 U" topped music charts worldwide and earned her widespread acclaim, including several prestigious awards.

Her fame soared, and Sinéad O'Connor became a household name. Her honest and unapologetic approach to her artistry further endeared her to fans, as she fearlessly tackled social and political issues in her music. Her authenticity resonated with a generation hungry for sincerity and meaning in their music.

As her star ascended, she continued to release successful albums, each one a testament to her evolving artistry and willingness to explore new musical territories. From her ethereal ballads to passionate rock anthems, Sinéad's versatility as an artist was boundless.

Despite the immense success, she remained true to her roots and maintained a connection with her Irish heritage, infusing her music with elements of traditional folk sounds. This blend of heartfelt emotions and cultural richness only further captivated audiences worldwide.

CHAPTER THREE

Awards and Achievements

Sinéad O'Connor's remarkable talent and distinctive voice earned her numerous awards and accolades throughout her illustrious career. As a singer-songwriter who fearlessly delved into the depths of human emotions, her music left an indelible mark on the hearts of fans and critics alike.

In 1990, Sinéad reached the pinnacle of her success with the release of her second studio album, "I Do Not Want What I Haven't Got." The album's lead single, her iconic rendition of "Nothing Compares 2 U," catapulted her to global stardom and garnered critical acclaim. As a result, she received several prestigious awards, including three Grammy nominations in 1991.

The powerful and emotionally charged music video for "Nothing Compares 2 U" also received widespread recognition. The song's raw vulnerability, combined with Sinéad's tearful and hauntingly beautiful performance, struck a chord with audiences worldwide. The video earned several awards and nominations, further cementing her status as a groundbreaking artist.

Sinéad O'Connor's impact on the music world extended far beyond her iconic hit. Her 1992 album, "Am I Not Your Girl?," showcased her versatility as an artist, interpreting classic songs with her unique style. The album received acclaim and added to her growing list of accolades.

Over the years, Sinéad continued to garner recognition for her artistry and contributions to the music industry. Her bold and introspective album, "Universal Mother" (1994), received critical praise for its emotional depth and thoughtful songwriting.

Beyond music, Sinéad O'Connor's activism and advocacy also earned her admiration and respect. Her outspoken views on social and political issues, including women's rights and LGBTQ+ rights, garnered attention and solidified her status as an artist with a strong sense of social responsibility.

While her career had its ups and downs, Sinéad O'Connor's undeniable talent and unwavering dedication to her craft resulted in a string of accolades and achievements. From Grammy nominations to music video awards, her work left an indelible impact on the music industry and continues to inspire artists and audiences worldwide.

CHAPTER FOUR

Relationships and Personal Life

Sinead O'Connor's personal life has been marked by a series of relationships that have shaped her journey as an artist, mother, and individual. Through love and loss, she navigated the complexities of romance, motherhood, and self-discovery, leaving an enduring impact on those closest to her.

Her first marriage was to music producer John Reynolds, and their union brought forth a son, Jake Reynolds, born in 1987. Although the marriage ultimately ended in divorce, their relationship endured beyond the dissolution of their romantic bond as they continued to co-parent their son, fostering a strong and supportive environment for Jake's growth and development.

In the following years, Sinead's path crossed with journalist John Waters, with whom she had a daughter named Roisin Waters, born in 1996. The relationship with John Waters also came to an end, but their shared commitment to their daughter's well-being remained steadfast, showcasing a dedication to parenthood even in times of change.

Sinead's journey towards motherhood continued when she welcomed her third child, Yeshua Francis Neil Bonadio, in 2006, with her partner Frank Bonadio. The experience of becoming a mother again offered her a renewed sense of purpose and love.

Tragically, in 2004, Sinead experienced the

devastating loss of her son, Shane O'Connor, born in 2004, whom she shared with musician Donal Lunny. Shane's passing in 2022, at the young age of 17, cast a profound shadow on Sinead's life. In the face of this heartbreak, she publicly grappled with her grief, openly sharing her struggles with loss and mental health, shining a light on the harsh realities of dealing with profound personal challenges.

Throughout her relationships and personal life, Sinead O'Connor's journey has been one of resilience, growth, and love. Despite the complexities and difficulties she faced, she demonstrated a fierce devotion to her children, seeking to provide them with a stable and nurturing environment, even amidst her own struggles. Her experiences as a mother and partner have informed her music, her activism, and her deep sense of empathy for others.

CHAPTER FIVE

Life in Politics and Activism

Sinead O'Connor's life in politics and activism is a testament to the power of using one's voice for social change. Throughout her career, she fearlessly tackled pressing issues and lent her support to causes close to her heart, becoming a force for advocacy and social justice.

her platform to bring attention to social and political matters. In 1992, during a live performance on "Saturday Night Live," she shocked the world by tearing up a picture of Pope John Paul II, denouncing the Catholic Church's handling of child abuse cases. This act of protest sparked debates on freedom of expression, religion, and accountability.

Unafraid of the repercussions, Sinead stood firm in her beliefs, using her prominence to advocate for women's rights and gender equality. She challenged societal norms and advocated for the empowerment of women, promoting dialogue on issues often considered taboo.

Her activism extended to her music as well. In her poignant song "Black Boys on Mopeds," she addressed issues of racial injustice and police brutality, using her art to shed light on systemic inequalities faced by minority communities.

O'Connor's advocacy work also encompassed LGBTQ+ rights, as she championed for the acceptance and equality of individuals from diverse sexual orientations and gender identities. She became a vocal ally, fighting for the rights and recognition of LGBTQ+ individuals during a time when such advocacy was not as common in the mainstream.

In addition to her vocal activism, O'Connor actively engaged in humanitarian efforts. She worked with organizations tackling issues such as homelessness and poverty, using her influence to raise awareness and funds for those in need.

Her willingness to be candid about her struggles with mental health further highlighted the urgency of addressing mental health issues and reducing stigma. By sharing her personal journey, she encouraged conversations on mental well-being and the importance of accessible support systems.

CHAPTER SIX

Controversies and Public Outbursts

Sinead O'Connor's career was punctuated by controversies and public outbursts that showcased the unyielding spirit of an artist unafraid to challenge societal norms and express her convictions.

In 1992, during a live performance on "Saturday Night Live," O'Connor shocked the world when she tore up a picture of Pope John Paul II while singing the word "evil." The act was a bold protest against the Catholic Church's handling of child abuse cases, and it ignited a firestorm of criticism and debate.

While some praised her bravery, others condemned the gesture as disrespectful and sacrilegious. The incident led to her being heavily scrutinized by the media and triggered a backlash that would have lasting effects on her career.

Following the Pope incident, O'Connor was scheduled to perform on "Late Show with David Letterman." However, her appearance was canceled after she refused to apologize for her actions. This further intensified the media frenzy and stirred debates about the boundaries of artistic expression and freedom of speech.

Throughout her career, O'Connor's outspoken views on social and political issues often landed her in contentious situations. Her activism for women's rights and gender equality earned both admiration and criticism. She fearlessly challenged societal norms, sparking heated discussions and public debates on topics that were considered taboo at the time.

In her music, O'Connor was unafraid to address sensitive subjects, leading to controversies over her song lyrics and music videos. For instance, her song "Black Boys on Mopeds" addressed issues of racial injustice and police brutality, raising awareness about systemic inequalities faced by minority communities. While praised by some for its thought-provoking nature, the song faced pushback from critics who felt it was too provocative.

Moreover, O'Connor's candidness about her struggles with mental health brought attention to the importance of mental health awareness. However, her emotional outbursts and public statements about her personal challenges also led to concerns about her well-being and raised questions about the responsibilities of the media and society in handling mental health issues.

Despite the controversies, O'Connor remained steadfast in her beliefs and used her platform to advocate for causes she deemed crucial. Her outspoken nature and willingness to challenge authority served as a reminder of the power artists have to effect change and provoke thought.

CHAPTER SEVEN

Personal Struggles

Behind the powerful voice and fearless persona, Sinead O'Connor's life was a poignant tale of personal struggles and mental health battles that touched the very core of her being.

Throughout her career, O'Connor openly shared her experiences with mental health issues, shining a light on the often stigmatized topic. In 1999, she was diagnosed with bipolar disorder, a condition marked by extreme mood swings and emotional turbulence. Herdiagnosis came after years of grappling with inner demons that she bravely confronted through her music and activism.

Despite her immense talent and success, the weight of fame took its toll on O'Connor's mental well-being. The relentless media scrutiny and public pressure magnified her struggles, making it challenging for her to find solace and peace.

In 2012, she made headlines after publicly expressing suicidal thoughts, revealing the depth of her pain and vulnerability. Her admission sparked concern among fans and the public, prompting discussions about the importance of mental health support for artists in the limelight.

Tragically, in 2022, O'Connor faced an unimaginable loss when her 17-year-old son, Shane O'Connor, died by suicide. The devastating event left her grappling with grief and intensified her advocacy for mental health awareness and suicide prevention.

Through it all, O'Connor's music served as an outlet for her emotions, allowing her to lay bare her struggles and triumphs. Songs like "Famine" and "8 Good Reasons" reflected her battles with depression and the complexities of her inner world. By sharing her pain, she connected with listeners who found solace in her raw honesty and vulnerability.

Despite the turbulence in her life, O'Connor's resilience shone through. She sought professional help and underwent therapy to manage her mental health challenges, demonstrating her commitment to healing and growth.

CHAPTER EIGHT

Sinead O'Connor Passes

On July 26, 2023, the world mourned the loss of an iconic voice as news spread of Sinead O'Connor's passing at the age of 56. Her departure left a void in the music industry and in the hearts of her devoted fans, who had been captivated by her soul-stirring performances and unyielding spirit for decades.

The news of her death reverberated across the globe, sparking an outpouring of grief and tributes from fellow musicians, fans, and public figures. Social media platforms were flooded with messages expressing gratitude for O'Connor's contributions to the world of music and activism.

Her legacy as a trailblazer in both realms was evident in the heartfelt tributes from artists she had inspired. Musicians praised her unique voice, raw authenticity, and fearlessness in tackling social and political issues through her music. Her impact extended beyond her iconic hit "Nothing Compares 2 U"; she was celebrated for her ability to use her art as a force for change and empowerment.

Her advocacy for mental health awareness resonated deeply with those who had faced similar struggles. Many shared stories of how O'Connor's openness about her own battles had given them courage to confront their own mental health challenges and seek help.

As the news of her passing spread, fans gathered

at impromptu memorials, leaving flowers, candles, and notes expressing their love and appreciation for the artist who had touched their lives. The collective mourning was a testament to the profound connection O'Connor had forged with her audience through her vulnerability and unyielding honesty.

Throughout her career, O'Connor's personal struggles had been laid bare for the world to witness. Her authenticity had endeared her to fans, who saw her not just as a music icon, but as a relatable human being navigating the complexities of life.

Tributes poured in from all corners of the world, celebrating the legacy of a woman who had left an indelible mark on music, activism, and mental health advocacy. Her music would continue to be a source of comfort and inspiration for generations to come.

CHAPTER NINE

Legacy and Impact

Sinead O'Connor's legacy is one of immense impact that transcends the boundaries of music and activism. As a trailblazing artist, she left an indelible mark on the world with her powerful voice, unapologetic spirit, and unwavering commitment to social justice and mental health advocacy.

Her impact on the music industry was profound. From her breakout hit "Nothing Compares 2 U" to her thought-provoking albums that challenged societal norms, O'Connor's music was a force to be reckoned with. Her unique vocal style and emotionally charged performances resonated deeply with audiences worldwide, earning her critical acclaim and numerous awards.

Beyond the charts, O'Connor's fearlessness in addressing pressing social and political issues through her music made her an influential figure in the realm of activism. She used her platform to advocate for women's rights, gender equality, LGBTQ+ rights, and racial justice, sparking important conversations on topics often considered taboo.

Her act of tearing up a picture of Pope John Paul II on "Saturday Night Live" in 1992 remains an enduring symbol of her unyielding spirit and commitment to speaking truth to power. It was a moment that sparked both controversy and discussions about freedom of expression and accountability.

O'Connor's openness about her struggles with

mental health also had a profound impact. By candidly sharing her experiences, she helped destigmatize mental illness and encouraged others to seek support and understanding. Her advocacy work highlighted the urgent need for mental health awareness and the importance of compassion in dealing with mental health challenges.

Her legacy is evident in the artists she inspired. Musicians and activists around the world have cited O'Connor as an influence on their own careers and advocacy efforts. Her willingness to use her fame to amplify marginalized voices and shed light on important issues set a precedent for artists using their platform for positive change.

Printed in Great Britain
by Amazon